Daniel O'Reilly

PYTHON FOR

DATA SCIENCE

The Ultimate Step-by-Step Guide to
Python Programming. Learn How to
Master Big Data Analysis and
Understand Machine Learning

Table of Contents

Introduction 6

Chapter 1: What is Data Science and how it works ... 8

Chapter 2: The Basics Of Data Science 14

Chapter 3: Data Science Libraries 32

Chapter 4: Most Frameworks for Python Data Science

.... 40

Chapter 5: How to process and understand data ... 82

Conclusion 106

Introduction

There is a lot of buzz in the business world, no matter what industry it is, about machine learning, the Python language, of data science, and being able to put these together and learn how they work can make a big difference for present and future business success. There are already a ton of companies out there who have been able to gain a competitive edge with data science and the various models and algorithms of Python that go with it. You can as well.

When you are ready to learn more about Python data science and what it can do for you and your business, make sure to check out this guidebook to get started.

There are so many different parts that come together when we work on data science. If you can put it all together and analyze the information to beat the competition, you will find that data science with Python can be the right move for you.

With the right coding language ready and some good data science libraries, there are a few more topics that we need to discuss when it comes to working with data science. We will look at some of the common tasks that we can do with data science, the different data types that work with here, and the future of data science and where this industry is going to head in the future, and what we should expect.

There is so much that we can do when it comes to working with data science and all of the information that comes in our data. Moreover, with the help of the Python coding language, we can learn how to make the right models and more to make all of this come together. When we are ready to learn more about Python data science and what it can do for us, make sure to check out this guidebook to get started.

With so many books made for this very subject, we are so happy you chose this one! We promise we made this book with the intention of making sure all information is as useful and enjoyable as possible. Happy reading!

Chapter 1:

What is Data Science and how it works

D ata science is likely a term that you have heard about at least a few times. If you are running a company, and you have ever taken a look at some of the steps that you can take in order to make yourself more efficient and to reduce the risks that you are experiencing when it is time to make some big and important decisions, then you have most likely heard about data science from others who are in the same boat as you. But this doesn't really explain that much about data science and what we can do with it. And that is where this guidebook is going to come into play. As the world started to enter the era of big data, the need for the right storage to use with it was something else that seemed to grow exponentially too. This was actually one of the main challenges and concerns that happen with these industries, at least until a few years ago. The main focus because of this issue was that companies might be able to collect and use a lot of data for their needs, they didn't have a good place to store all of that data to work with later. Now, thanks to some of the changes that are there in the technology that we have, this is no longer the big issue that it was in the past. This means that we can make a few adjustments and work with more and more data in the process.

You will find that the secret sauce that is going to bring it all together, help us gather the data that we need, and will ensure that we are able to learn from data insights is data science.

There are a lot of companies that are looking to get into the world of data science because they know all of the benefits that come with this. When we are ready to handle some of the data that is going on with all of this, we need to make sure that we are getting the right data, and that we actually understand all of the information at the same time. But that is all going to be covered in data analysis that we are doing along the way.

Why is Data Science So Important?

The first thing that we need to take a look at is why data science is so important, and why a company may need to work with the process of data science along the way. The first issue is the way that this data has been structured in our modern world, especially when it is compared to how it was done in the past. Traditionally, the data that companies were able to get their hands on was going to be smaller in size, and it was pretty much structured the whole time. This allowed us to work with simple business intelligence tools in order to analyze what is going on.

However, this is not the case any longer. There are benefits and downsides that come with this, of course. t allows us the option to really know more about a situation because we can really gather up the data and understand more with more data. But often this data is unstructured, and that makes it harder to sort through it and understand it as well.

Unlike the structured and easier-to-work-with data that was found in older, traditional systems, we will find that most of our data today is unstructured or at most semi-structured. This makes it harder to work with and can take longer to sort and analyze. But because we can find more information to help shape the decisions that we are making, this is not necessarily a bad thing all of the time.

This data is generated from a lot of different sources, including things like instruments, sensors, multimedia forms, text files, and even some financial logs along the way. Because of all these sources that we are getting the data from, it is important to see that we are not able to work with some of the simple business intelligence tools because they are not going to be capable of handling all of this data and the variety of data as well.

This is why it is important to know data science in order to work with algorithms and analytical tools that are more advanced and complex. This ensures that we can really analyze and derive meaningful insights from the data as well.

Of course, this is not going to be the only reason that data science is something that has become so popular. Let's dig deeper and see how data science is being used in a lot of different domains. For example, what if we can go through the data that we have, and we were then able to learn the precise requirements of the customers we have using a lot of the data that we have on these existing customers? This could include things like their income, age, purchase history, and past browsing history as well.

No doubt, you have been working with this kind of data already. But this doesn't mean that we had the right tools in order to handle some of this and get it all organized.

With the work of data science, though, it is possible to train the models in the most efficient manner and have some good precision when it is time to recommend products to your customers. All of this can be done with data science when you get started.

Based on all of the data that the car can gather, it can make decisions to help it drive, including when it should speed up or go slower when it should overtake another car, or even where to turn. With the help of data science and making use of advanced machine learning algorithms, this is done.

We can even work with data science in order to help out with the predictive analytics. For example, we can work with something like weather forecasting. Data from things like satellites, radars, aircraft, ships, and more can be analyzed in order to help us build up some of the models that we have.

These models are useful when we can forecast the weather, while also being able to predict the occurrence of any natural calamities that we would like. It is also going to help us to take some of the right measures ahead of time when we see this. In the process, it can help us save a lot of lives.

Chapter 2:

The Basics Of Data Science

The use of data science is becoming ever more prominent in many businesses and in a lot of different industries as well. But that doesn't really explain what data science is all about. We may want to figure out what it takes to do data analysis, what tools we need to make the predictions, and so much more. These are all questions that we will answer in this part of the guidebook to make things a bit easier.

First, we need to see what data science is. Data science is a blend of algorithms, tools, and principles that come with machine learning. All of these different things come together with the intention of discovering covert patterns from the raw data. How is this different from what we have seen statisticians doing for years now? The answer that lies in the difference between predicting and explaining something.

A data analyst is usually going to be a person who will explain what is taking place by preparing the history that comes with the data. But then a data scientist is a bit different because they are not only working through some of that exploratory analysis from above, but they are also going to use a lot of different algorithms of advanced machine learning to help them figure out how likely a certain event in the future is. A data scientist can take that data and look at is from a variety of angles, and hopefully, see it from a few other angles that were not explored in the past. There are actually a few different types of analyses and analytics to make some smart decisions and use the data that we have to our advantage.

How Can I Use Data Science?

One of the first things that we will have questions when it comes to data science is the idea of how we can use it. It may seem like a really neat thing to learn about just for fun, but there are actually quite a few practical purposes for using data science no matter what industry you are in or how you plan to use it. Some of the different ways that we can rely on data science will include the following considerations.

It can help with marketing

Marketing is all about data. When we use all of the big data that is needed for data science, we find that we can really learn more about our customers and how we can reach them to make a sale.

There are different ways that a company can use data science in order to help them get ahead of the game.

It can help in knowing how to reach the customers, placing heads in the right places for the right customers, etc.

Helps the company to learn more about their customers

As a company, the more that you can learn about your customers, the better off you are.

Learning about what your customers want out of your business, their demographics, and how you can serve them better will ensure that they will continue to choose your business, rather than working with someone else along the way.

It can even help you to determine which products you will sell next.

It can help to reduce waste

All companies want to le arn about and reduce the amount of waste that is going ton in their company. This waste can be resources, time, machine parts, and even part of the process of making the product. When we can cut down on some of this waste, it can help the company to become more efficient and will increase the profits that the company is going to experience. When you can use data science in the proper manner, you will find that it is easier to cut out some of this waste and see the results that you would like.

Financial institutions use it to help them fight off fraud

Fraud can cost these financial institutions a lot of money overall. If they are not careful with how they handle their money and they don't learn how to distinguish between fraudulent and legitimate transactions, there are some problems along the way. When a financial institution can come up with algorithms and programs that can recognize and stop fraud, it can end up saving them millions of dollars a year.

It can speed up loan applications

With the help of data science, the financial institution can go through the applications and figure out which loans are the best bets and not.

You can set up a few of the different criteria that the application needs to meet, and then work from there. If the application meets some of the requirements, then it is a good option to work with. The loan officer will get these and can make the final determination about it. But if the loan application doesn't meet the requirements, it will get ignored and not be seen at all. This helps to speed up the loan application process and can allow the loan officer a chance to keep up with their work and focus on the customers who will bring that financial institution money.

It helps out in the medical field in a variety of ways

There are so many ways that the process of data science would be able to help in the medical field. To start, we can see that data science will help out doctors finish their surgeries. With the use of machine learning and other algorithms that come with data science, doctors can make precise incisions, get the surgery done with minimal issues, and with less recovery time.

It helps a company learn more about their current competition and the industry they are in

When you have all of this information in place, you will find that it is easier to figure out what is working and what is not working.

You can then jump right in and make some of the necessary adjustments to your own business model. You may find a new way to reach your customers that no one else is working with. You may be able to make some modifications to a technique that someone else is working with that can improve your own business, as well.

Many manufacturing companies will work with data science because it allows them to make predictions that can save them money

First, you can use these kinds of algorithms to figure out when a part on a machine is likely to break, or when you need to do maintenance. Then, you can schedule this during the off-hours, ensuring that the machine is always up and running on time, and that production is not going to be halted while you figure things out.

These algorithms can also work, in pretty much any business when it is time to work with finding ways to cut down on some of the waste that is present. Every company is going to have some kind of waste. Figuring out how to reduce that waste and take care of it will enable you to offer the products at a competitive rate, while still making as much in profits as possible. It is simple to work with data science to figure out where the waste is and how you can keep it to a minimum.

When you are shopping online and see a recommendation tab on a website, you see some of the work of data science and machine learning coming to life.

These are popular on many websites because they can make it easier for the customer to make some informed decisions on what they want to watch next, purchase next, or something else. Businesses will enjoy them as well because with these recommendation systems, it is more likely that the customer is going to make another purchase, which is going to increase the bottomline for that company.

Next on the list is the process of speech recognition. If you have ever talked to or asked a question from your smartphone, or if you have worked with some of the popular devices like the Echo, Cortana, etc., then you can recognize how this feature is fun and innovative. It is run with some of the principles of data science.

In fact, some of the best examples that we will find when it comes to data science is this speech recognition. Using these features, even if you are not currently in a position to type out a message, you are still about to talk to the machine or the device and ask a question. However, this may not perform accurately, especially when we are at the beginning. This means that we may have to spend some time working with the program and teaching it how to recognize some of the things that we are saying. Machine learning is behind the process by which the machine, through experience and some time, can learn how to recognize the speech of the user faster and more efficiently.

If you have ever worked with some of the websites that are out there that help out with price comparisons, then you have seen data science at work as well. At a basic kind of level, you will find that these are websites driven with big data that they can get with the help of RSS Feeds and APIs. They can then use this information to figure out what the price of the same product from different websites and sources are, so you can make the best decision and save money. This can be used in many industries to help you compare prices and figure out what is best for you.

We can also take a look at how this kind of technology is going to work when we talk about something like airline route planning. This industry is one that isar a lot of heavy losses if people are not careful. Except for a few companies out there, many are struggling to maintain the occupancy that they need and make some profits. And when we add in the higher prices of fuel right now, and the need to offer heavy discounts to many customers, the situation is slowly getting worse.

It wasn't too long before these airline companies started to work with data science to see how they can increase their profits and make more without scaring their customers away. This helped them to figure out some of the strategic improvements that they can make. Today, with the help of data science, these airline companies can:

- Make better predictions about a flight being delayed

- Decide which class of airplanes they should invest their money in

- Whether they should land at the direct destination or take a halt in between

- Help to drive some of the loyalty programs that customers can sign up for

Two of the airline companies who have embraced these changes include American Airlines and Southwest Airlines, and they are now some of the most profitable of the airlines out there.

Companies like UPS, FedEx, and DHL will use data science to help improve operational efficiency.

With the help of data science, these companies and more have been able to figure out the best routes to ship, the best times that they should deliver, and the mode of transportation that is the best as well. This helps them to have more cost efficiency and other benefits along the way as well. In addition, the data that these companies can generate with the installed GPS units can provide them with the data they need to explore more possibilities, and to learn more with data science along the way.

There are so many benefits that we can see when it comes to using data science for a company. In many cases, if you are not willing to use data science at least a little bit, you will find that you will fall behind. No matter what kind of business problem you are trying to solve, you will find that working with data science is one of the best and most effective methods in helping you out.

Different Types of Data We Can Work With

There are two main types, mainly structured and unstructured. The types of algorithms and models that we can run on them will depend on what kind of data we are working with. Both can be valuable, but it often depends on what we are trying to learn, and which one will serve us the best for the topic at hand.

With that in mind, let's dive into some of the differences between structured and unstructured data, and why each can be so important to our data analysis.

Structured Data

The first type of data that we will explore is known as **structured** data. This is often the kind that is considered traditional data. This means that we will see it consisting mainly of lots of text files that are organized and have a lot of useful information. We can quickly glance through this information and see what kind of data is there, without having to look up for more information, label it, or look through videos to find what we want.

Structured data is the kind that we can store inside one of the options for warehouses of data. We can then pull it up any time that we want for analysis. Before the era of big data, and some of the emerging sources of data that we are using regularly now, structured data was the only option that most companies would use to make their business decisions.

Many companies still love to work with structured data. The data is very organized and easy to read through, and it is easier to digest. This ensures that our analysis is easier to go through with legacy solutions to data mining. To make this more specific, structured data is made up largely of some of basic customer data and could provide us with some information including the contact information, addresses, names, geographical locations, etc. of the customers.

In addition to all of this, a business may decide to collect some transactional data. This would be a source of structured data as well. Some of the transactional data that the company may choose to work with could include financial information, but we must make sure that when this is used, it is stored appropriately so it meets the standards of compliance for the industry.

There are several methods we can use to manage this structured data. For the most part, though, this type of data is managed with legacy solutions of analytics because it is already well organized, and we do not need to go through it and make adjustments and changes to the data. This can save a lot of time and hassle in the process, and it ensures that we will get the data that we want, to work the way that we want.

Of course, even with the rapid rise that we see with new sources of data, companies are still going to work at dipping into the stores of structured data that they have. This helps them to produce higher quality insights, ones that are easier to gather and will not be as hard to look through the model for insights either. These insights will help the company learn some of the new ways that they can run their business.

While companies that are driven by data all over the world have been able to analyze structured data for a long time, over many decades, they are just now starting to take some of the emerging sources of data as seriously as they should have. The good news though is that it is creating a lot of new opportunities in their company and is helping them to gain some of the momentum and success that they want.

Even with all of the benefits that come with structured data, this is often not the only source of data that companies will rely on. First off, finding this kind of data can take a lot of time and can be a waste if you need to get the results quickly and efficiently. Collecting structured data is something that takes some time, simply because it is so structured and organized.

Another issue that we need to watch out for when it comes to structured data is that it can be more expensive. It takes someone a lot of time to sort through and organize all of that data. While it may make the model that we are working on more efficient than other forms, it can often be expensive to work with this kind of data.

Companies need to balance their costs and benefits here and determine if they want to use any structured data at all. If they do, they need to decide how much of the structured data they will add to their model.

Unstructured Data

The next option of data that we can look at is known as **unstructured** data. This kind of data is a bit different than what we talked about before, but it is starting to grow in influence, as companies are trying to find ways to leverage the new and emerging data sources. Some companies choose to work with just unstructured data on their own, and others choose some mixture of unstructured and structured data. This provides them with some of the benefits of both. This can help them to get the answers they need to provide good customer service and other benefits to their business.

There are many sources where we can get these sources of data, but mainly they come from streaming data. Streaming data comes in from mobile applications, social media platforms, location services, and the Internet of Things. Since the prevalent diversity in unstructured sources of data, businesses that choose to use unstructured data will likely rely on many different sources. Businesses may find that it is harder to manage unstructured data than structured data.

Because of this trouble in managing unstructured data, there are many times when a company are challenged by this data, in ways that they weren't in the past. Many times, they have to add in some creativity to handle the data and make sure they are pulling out the relevant data, from all of those sources for their analytics.

The growth and the maturity of things known as data lakes, and even the platform, known as Hadoop, are a direct result of the expanding collection of unstructured data. Traditional environments that were used with structured data are not going to cut it at this point, and they are not going to be a match when it comes to the unstructured data that most companies want to collect and analyze now.

Because it is hard to handle the new sources and types of data, we can't use the same tools and techniques that we did in the past. Companies who want to work with unstructured data have to pour additional resources into various programs and human talent in order to handle the data and collect relevant insights and data from it.

The lack of any structure that is easily defined inside this type of data can sometimes turn businesses away from this kind of data in the first place. But there is a lot of potential that is hidden in that data. We just need to learn the right methods to use to pull that data out. The unstructured data is certainly going to keep the data scientist busy overall because they can't just take the data and record it in a data table or a spreadsheet. But with the right tools and a specialized set of skills to work with, those who are trying to use unstructured data to find the right insights, and are willing to make some investments in time and money, will find that it can be so worth it in the end.

Both of these types of data, the structured and the unstructured, are important when it comes to the success you see with your business. Sometimes our project just needs one or the other of these data types, and other times it needs a combination of both.

For a company to reach success though, they need to be able to analyze, properly and effectively, all of their data, regardless of the type of the source. Given the experience that the enterprise has with data, it is not a big surprise that all of this buzz already surrounds data that comes from sources that may be seen as unstructured.

As new technologies begin to surface that can help enterprises of all sizes analyze their data in one place, it is more important than ever for us to learn what this kind of data is all about and how to combine it with some of the more traditional forms of data, including structured data.

The Components of Data Science

Now, we also need to take some time to look at the basics of data science.

There are a few key components that come into play when we are talking about data science. Having these in place is going to make a big difference in how well we can handle some of the different parts that come with data science, and how we can take on some of the different parts that we need with our own projects.

Some of the key components that we need to take a look at when it comes to data science will include:

The various types of data

The foundation of any data science project is the raw set of data. There are a lot of different types. We can work with the structured data that is mostly found in tabular form, and the unstructured data, which is going to include PDF files, emails, videos, and images.

Programming

You will need some kind of programing language to get the work done, with Python and R being the best options. Data management and data analysis are done with computer programming. Python and R are the two most popular programming languages that we will focus on here.

Statistics and probability

Data is manipulated in different ways to extract some good information out of it. The mathematical foundation of data science is probability and statistics. Without having a good knowledge of the probability and statistics, there is a higher possibility of misinterpreting the data and reaching conclusions that are not correct. This is a big reason why probability and statistics are so important in data science.

Machine learning

As someone who is working with data science, each day you will spend at least a little time learning the algorithms of machine learning. This can include methods of classification and regression. A data scientist needs to know machine learning to complete their job since this is the tool that is needed to help predict valuable insights from the available data.

Big data

In our current world, raw data is what we use to train and test our models, and then figure out the best insights and predictions out of that data. Working with big data can help us to figure out what important (even hidden) information is found in our raw data. There are a lot of different tools that we can use to help us not only find the big data but also to process big data.

Many companies are learning the value of data science and all that comes with it. They like the idea that they can take data they have been collecting for a long period and put it to use to increase their business for a competitive edge. In the rest of this guidebook, we will spend some time focusing on how to work with data science and all of the different parts that come with it as well.

Chapter 3:
Data Science Libraries

N ow that we know a bit about the basics that come with the Python language, we must spend some time learning the best libraries and extensions that we can add into the mix, to make sure that Python is going to work the way that we would like for data science. The regular library that comes with Python can do a lot of amazing things, but it is not going to be able to handle all of the graphing, mathematics, and machine learning that we need from data science.

The good news here though is that there are a few other libraries that we can work with that utilize Python and help with machine learning and data science together. All of these will help us handle tasks in a slightly different manner, so take a look at them and how they are meant to work with Python and data science. The best libraries that can help you to get this work done will include the following:

NumPy and SciPy

If you want to do any kind of work with machine learning or data science in Python, you have to make sure that you work with the NumPy and the SciPy library.

Both of these are the basis of many other libraries we will talk about here, which is why it is likely that when you work with data science, you will also add in a bit of library help as well.

First, we will look at NumPy, which stands for Numeric and Scientific Computation. This is a useful library because it lays down some of the basic premises that we need for doing any kind of scientific computing in Python. This library can also help us get ahold of some functions that have been precompiled for us. It is fast for handling any numerical and mathematical routine processes that you would like to do.

Then, there is also the Scientific Python library, which we call SciPy, that goes along with NumPy in many cases. This is the kind of library that you want to work with to add in some kind of competitive edge to your work in machine learning. This happens when you work to enhance some of the useful functions for things like regression and minimization, to name a few.

Theano

Theano is the next library that we can take a look at. It spends some more time working in a process known as deep learning, rather than just machine learning. Theano is a package from Python that will define some of the multi-dimensional arrays, similar to what we see with the NumPy library above, along with some of the math operations and expressions.

This particular library is compiled, which makes sure that it is going to run as efficiently as possible on all architectures that you choose along the way. it was originally developed by the Machine Learning group of University de Montreal. It is used to help us handle a lot of the applications that we want to complete in machine learning.

The most important thing that we need to look at when it comes to working with this library is that Theano can tightly integrate with the NumPy library on some of the operations that are at the lower level. The library will also optimize the use of CPU and GPU when you are working, which ensures that the performance that we will see in data-intensive computation is even faster than before. The stability and the efficiency that come with this library will allow us to receive more precise results, even when we are talking about smaller values.

Matplotlib

As you are going through data science and Python, there are times when you will want to work with a graph, chart, or some other kind of visual. This is going to make it easier to see the information that is found in the text at a glance. Matplotlib can make some of these graphs for you in no time.

The Matplotlib extension is going to provide us with all of the parts that we need to take the information and turn it into visualizations that you need for your data.

This library is going to work with pretty much any type of visualization that you need—a histogram, bar chart, error chart, line graph, and more.

The Scikit-Learn library

The Scikit-Learn is a great one to go with when it comes to machine learning. This is because the package that comes with this library provides us with many machine learning algorithms and more that we can use to get data science to work. It is going to include many different parts that can ensure we analyze the information that is fed into the algorithm properly.

One other benefit that we will see when it comes to this kind of library is that it is easy to distribute, which means it works well in commercial and academic settings, and there are not a lot of dependencies that go with it. The interface is concise and consistent, which makes it easier to work with, and you will find that the most common of the machine learning algorithms are already inside, making it easier to create some of the models you need for data science.

Pandas

The next library in Python that you want to work with to make machine learning and data science do what you would like is Pandas. Pandas stands for the Python Data Analysis Library, which helps us to do a lot of the work that is needed in the Python world. This is an open-source tool that helps us with some of the data structures that are needed to do data analysis. You can use this library to add in the right tools and data structures to make sure your data analysis is complete. Many industries like to work with this one to help out in different areas like finance, statistics, engineering, and social science.

The Pandas library is adaptable which makes it great for getting a ton of work done in less time. It can also help you work with any kind of data that you can bring in, no matter what kind of source you are getting that information from, making it a lot easier to work with. This library is going to come with many different features that you can enjoy. Some of the best ones will include:

You can use the Pandas library to help reshape the structures of your data.

You can use the Pandas library to label series, as well as tabular data, to help us see an automatic alignment.

You can use the Pandas library to help with heterogeneous indexing of the information. it is also useful when it comes to systematic labeling of the data as well.

You can use this library because it can hold onto the capabilities of identifying and then fixing any data that is missing.

This library provides us with the ability to load and then save data from more than one format.

You can easily take some of the data structures that come out of Python and NumPy and convert the objects you need into Pandas objects.

TensorFlow

TensorFlow, one of the best Python libraries for data science, is a library that was released by Google Brain. It was written mostly in the language of C++ but it is going to include some bindings in Python, so the performance is not something that you will need to worry about. One of the best features that come with this library is some of the flexible architecture that is found in the mix, which is going to allow the programmer to deploy it with one or more GPUs or CPUs in a desktop, mobile, or server device while using the same API the whole time. This library is also unique in that it was developed by the Google Brain project, and it is not used by many other programmers. However, you do need to spend a bit more time to learn the API compared to some of the other libraries. In just a few minutes, you will find that it is possible to work with the TensorFlow library to implement the design of your network, *without* having to fight through the API as you do with other options.

The Keras library

If you are looking for a Python library that can handle data science and enables data analytics that are also easy for the user to work with, then this is the library for you. It can handle a lot of the different processes that come with the other libraries, but it keeps in mind the user, rather than the machine when it comes to designing the interface and the other parts that you use within this coding library. The user experience is easy, the interface is designed to only need a few clicks to get the processes done, and it all comes together to make data science and machine learning as easy as possible.

This library is going to work a lot of the modules that are needed for machine learning. You can work with a module that is on its own, or you can combine a few modules to get the results that you would like. There is a lot of flexibility that comes with using this kind of library. That is one of the many reasons that so many programmers like to use it when completing work with Python data science.

These are just a few of the different libraries that you can use along with the Python coding language to get some of your data science and machine learning work done. These libraries all work on slightly different types of processes when it comes to data science, which is going to make them so much easier to work with overall. Take a look at each one and see just how they can all come together to provide you with the results that you want in your data analytics project.

We need to take some time to peruse through some of the best libraries that we can use when it comes to working with the Python language and data science.

The standard Python library can do a lot of amazing things. But when it is time to make some of the models that you would like with machine learning and more, the standard library is going to lack a few of the capabilities that you would like to work with.

This is why we would need to bring in some additional extensions and libraries to the mix. You will find that Python has a lot of different libraries that can handle the data, and the different models that you want to handle overall. You just need to pick out which one is going to work for the projects you have in mind. Some can help out with all of the different types of tasks that you want to handle, and some will do better with certain algorithms or models that we want to work with.

These libraries are critical when it is time to handle the algorithms and the models that are needed. Without them, you will miss out on some of the tasks that are needed to help with data science. It will make it more difficult to create models that help you with predictions and more. There are a lot of different libraries that you can work with when it is time to handle machine learning, deep learning, and data science.

Chapter 4:

Most Frameworks for

Python Data Science

Working with NumPy

N ow it is time for us to take a look at one of the great libraries that we can work with when it comes to using Python and getting our data analysis to work for our needs. NumPy is one of the first that we can look at, and it is one of the best. It is actually going to be the basis of what we see in some of the other important libraries that we will discuss later on, or in other data analysis libraries, so it is worth our time to take a look at it.

To start, NumPy is a library that is used in Python. We can use it for several different reasons including numerical as well as scientific computing, if we need it. For the most part, though, it is used to help us compute our arrays quickly and efficiently. We will have it based and written out in Python and the C language.

Even though this is a language that works for the C language as well, this is a basic data analysis library that we will use with Python, and the word 'NumPy' is going to stand for Numerical

Python. We will bring out this library to help us to process any of the homogeneous multidimensional arrays that we want to handle.

This library is one of the core libraries that are used for different scientific computations. This means that it is going to have a powerful array of multidimensional objects, and it will integrate some tools that are useful when it is time to work with these arrays as well.

You will quickly find that when you work with the data analysis that we have been talking about, NumPy is useful in almost all of the scientific programming that we try to do with Python, including things like statistics, machine learning, and bioinformatics. It is also going to provide us with some good functions that we can work with, functions that can work well and run efficiently, and is well written in the process.

As we mentioned before, this is a library that is focused mainly on performing some of the mathematical operations that we need to use on contiguous arrays, much like the arrays that are found in a few other languages, including what is seen in the C language. This means that we can use NumPy to help us manipulate some of our numerical data as well

This library is really basic, but it is still going to be important when it comes to handling some of the scientific computing that we want to do with Python.

Plus, it will not take that long working with data science and data analysis before you find that this is the library that other data analysis libraries are dependent on.

Some of the other major libraries are dependent on the arrays in NumPy as their inputs and outputs. In addition to this, it is also going to provide some functions that will allow developers to perform all of the basic and the advanced functions that they would like, (whether we are talking about statistics or mathematics), and especially when we are dealing with multidimensional arrays and matrices, without needing to use as many lines of codes to get it all done.

When we compare these arrays with the lists that we talked about earlier with Python, you will find that the arrays are much faster. But Python lists do have an advantage over the arrays because they are more flexible, as you are only able to store the same data type in each column when you are working with the arrays.

There are a few features that you will enjoy when it is time to work with the NumPy library. Some of the main features that you will enjoy the most will include:

The NumPy library is a combination of Python and C language

This is going to consist of arrays that are homogeneous and multidimensional. Ndarray is part of this as well, which are n-dimensional arrays as well.

It is going to work on a lot of different functions for arrays if you would like.

It can also help us to reshape the arrays. It also allows Python to have a way to work as an alternative to MATLAB.

There are a lot of reasons why we would want to work with NumPy rather than having to pick one of the other libraries that are out there along the way. We will use the array in NumPy for the work that we are doing in Python instead of a list. Some of the reasons for this include it is convenient to work with, it is going to perform faster than other methods, and it is going to use less memory overall.

All of these are important when we are trying to do some of the algorithms that we need in data analysis. And mostly, you will notice that the arrays are the number one thing that we utilize when it is time to work with this library as well.

There are a few other things that we need to explore when it comes to how we can work with the NumPy library. First, the NumPy array is going to take up a lot less space than other options.

On the other hand, we can create an array, it is only going to take about 4 MB. If you need to use a lot of different arrays as you go through, and they will fit better on the space of your memory overall. Arrays are also going to be easier to access when you would like to read, and write on them later on.

In addition, the performance when it comes to speed, you will find that the NumPy arrays are great. It can perform a lot faster when it comes to computations than what we find with the Python lists. Because this library is considered open-sourced, it is not going to cost you anything to get started with. Then it also has the benefit of working with the popular Python programming language, which has high-quality libraries for almost all of the tasks that you want to accomplish.

All of these are great benefits to work with. You will find that it is a high-quality library that is going to help us to get things done. You can get it to match up with the libraries that you want, it is free to work with, and it can handle a lot of the data analysis projects that you want to do. It is also an easy library that will connect some of the codes that already exist in the C language over to the interpreter for Python, so you can get your work done.

There are a lot of benefits that will come up when you want to work with the NumPy library, and you will find that it is the basis for a lot of the codes and algorithms that you want to write out when you are analyzing data. Learning how to use this language and what it can do for you is going to make a world of difference in how much you can accomplish for the long-term. It is worth your time to learn more about it as well to complete your project.

The n-Dimensional Array

You can build complex data structures with them because they are powerful at storing data. However, they're not great at operating on that data. They aren't optimal when it comes to processing power and speed, which are critical when working with complex algorithms. This is why we're using NumPy and its ndarray object, which stands for an "n-dimensional array." Let's look at the properties of a NumPy array.

It is optimal and fast at transferring data. When you work with complex data, you want the memory to handle it efficiently instead of being bottlenecked.

You can perform vectorization. In other words, you can make linear algebra computations and specific element operations without being forced to use for loops.

This is a large plus side for NumPy because Python for loops cost a lot of resources, thereby making it expensive to work with a large number of loops instead of ndarrays.

In data science operations you will have to use tools, or libraries, such as SciPy and Scikit-learn. You can't use them without arrays because they are required as an input, otherwise functions won't perform as intended.

With that being said, here are a few methods of creating a ndarray:

- Take an already existing data structure and turn it into an array.

- Build the array from the start and add in the values later.

- You can also upload data to an array even when it's stored on a disk.

Converting a list to a one-dimensional array is a fairly common operation in data science processes. Keep in mind that you have to take into account the type of objects such a list contains. This will have an impact on the dimensionality of the result. Here's an example of this with a list that contains only integers: In: import numpy as np

int_list = [1,2,3]

Array_1 = np.array(int_list)

In: Array_1

Out: array([1, 2, 3])

You can access the array just like you access a list in Python. Simply use indexing; just like in Python, it starts from 0. This is how this operation would look: In: Array_1[1]

Out: 2

Now you can gain more data about the objects inside the array, like so:

In: type(Array_1)

Out: numpy.ndarray

In: Array_1.dtype

Out: dtype('int64')

The result of the dtype is related to the type of operating system you're running. In this example, we're using a 64-bit operating system.

At the end of this exercise, our basic list is transformed into a uni-dimensional array. But what happens if we have a list that contains more than just one type of element? Let's say we have integers, strings, and floats. Let's see an example of this: In: import numpy as np

composite_list = [1,2,3] + [1.,2.,3.] + ['a','b','c']

Array_2 = np.array(composite_list[:3])#here we have only integers

print ('composite_list[:3]', Array_2.dtype)

Array_2 = np.array(composite _list[:6]) #now we have integers and floats

print (' composite _list[:6]', Array_2.dtype)

Array_2 = np.array(composite _list) #strings have been added to the array

print (' composite _list[:] ',Array_2.dtype)

Out:

composite _list[:3] int64

composite _list[:6] float64

composite _list[:] <U32

As you can see, we have a "composite_list" that contains integers, floats, and strings. It's important to understand that when we make an array, we can have any data types and mix them however we wish.

Next, let's see how we can load an array from a file. N-dimensional arrays can be created from the data contained inside a file.

Here's an example in code: In: import numpy as np

cars = np.loadtxt('regression-datasets

cars.csv',delimiter=',', dtype=float)

In this example, we tell our tool to create an array from a file with the help of the "loadtxt" method—by giving it a filename, delimiter, and a data type.

Manipulating Our Arrays

Now, it is time for us to take a look at how we can work with some of the arrays that are in our midst and how these are important in unlocking some of the features of arrays and the NumPy library.

Like many other data science libraries that are out there and Python as well, NumPy is one of the packages that we just can't miss out on, especially when it is time to learn more about data science along the way. This is because NumPy can provide us with some of the data structure that we need with arrays that will hold a few benefits over the list with Python. For example, the arrays are more compact. They can access faster when it is time to read and write the items, and overall they are more efficient and convenient to work with.

With this in mind, we will spend some time looking at how to work with the NumPy arrays. We will look at how to work with these, how they can be installed, and how to make some of the arrays, even when you need to work with the data when it is on the files.

Working with Matplotlib

This is one of the best plotting libraries that you can use in Python, especially when you would like to handle things like 2D graphics.

It can be used with a lot of other different places, like on the web application servers, Python shell, Python script, and some other toolkits out there that have graphical user interfaces.

There are some toolkits available that will help to extend out some of the functions that we will see with Matplotlib and will ensure that we can do some more with this program in no time at all. Some of these will include us going through a separate download.

Others are found with the source code of this library but will have to depend on a few other aspects that are not found in Python or this library. Some of the different extensions that we can focus on and can work with when it is time to extend what Matplotlib can do will include:

Basemap

This is a map-plotting toolkit that can be helpful if this is what you would like to do. It is a good option to use if you would like to work with political boundaries, coastlines, and even some map projections overall.

Natgrid

This is an interface that goes to the Natgrid library. This is best when we want to handle something like the irregular gridding of the spaced data that we have.

Mplot3d

This is helpful when you would like to extend out the 2D functions of Matplotlib into something that is more 3D in nature.

Excel tools

This library provides some utilities that we need to exchange data with Microsoft Excel if we need it.

Cartopy

This is one of the mapping libraries that we can work with that will help us in some of the definitions of map projections and some of the arbitrary point, line, polygon, and image transformation capabilities to name a few of the features. There are a lot of the different options that we can work with along the way. It is good for handling most of the features that we would like to see, and most of the graphs that are important when it comes to this kind of data science. For example, you may find that this library is going to work well when we want to handle things like pie charts, line graphs, histograms, bar graphs, area plots, scatter plots, and more. If you need to create your own chart or graph to go through some of the data that you are handling during this time, then working with the Matplotlib library is one of the best options. It does lack some of the 3D features that you may need, so this is something to consider based on your data.

But for some of the basic parts that you would like to add into the mix and for most of the visuals that you would like to focus on, you will find that the Matplotlib library can handle it in no time.

How to Work with Matplotlib to Create Great Visuals

Another great library that we can work with, especially when we are spending some time working on our own visuals as we talked about before, is the Matplotlib library. This is a great option to work with when we handle some of the work that we want to do with a data science project. It will ensure that we can take all of the data points and different predictions from algorithms to help us with visuals, so that we understand the data a little bit easier. To start with, Matplotlib is one of the plotting libraries that are available to work along with the Python programming language. It is also going to be one of the components that come with the NumPy library, big data, and some of the numerical handling resources. Matplotlib uses an API that is more object-oriented in order to help embed plots in applications of Python as well. Since Python is used in machine learning in many cases, resources like NumPy and Matplotlib are used in many cases to help out with some of the modeling that we need to do with machine learning, and to ensure that we can work with these technologies either.

The idea that we will get with this one is that the programmer can access these libraries to handle some of the key tasks that are inside of the bigger environment of Python. It is then able to go through and integrate the results with all of the other elements and features of the program for machine learning, a neural network, and some of the other more advanced options that we would like to use.

You will also find that some of the utility that we can see with this library, as well as with the NumPy library is centered around numbers. The utility of Matplotlib is specifically done with visual plotting tools.

So, in a sense, these resources are going to be more analytical rather than generative. However, all of the infrastructures that we can see with this library is going to allow for the programs of machine learning, when we correctly use them, can give us the right results for human handlers as well.

With some of this information in mind, we need to look a bit more into the Matplotlib library. To start with, this is part of the package from Python that helps with 2D graphics. Learning how to work with this kind of library efficiently is so important when you would like to handle some of the visuals and even more that you want to do in a data science project.

Data Visualization and Matplotlib

At some point in your journey to working with all of that data and trying to analyze it, you will decide that it is time to visualize the data. Sure, we could put all of that information into a table or write it out in long and boring paragraphs, but this is going to make it hard to focus and see the comparisons and more that come with that information. One of the best ways to do this is to take that information, and after it has been analyzed accurately, we can use data visualization to get this to work for our needs.

The good news is that the Matplotlib library, which is an extension of NumPy and SciPy, can help us create all of them. Whether you want to look at your data as a line graph, a pie chart, a histogram, or some other form, the Matplotlib library is there to help.

The first thing that we will try and explore when it comes to this topic is data visualization. We need to have a better idea of what data visualization is all about, how it works, why we would want to use it, and so on. When we can put all of these parts together, it becomes much easier to take all of that data we have been collecting, and then actually see it in a way that is easy to look over and make smart business decisions with.

These are just a few of the examples of the data visualization that you may encounter as you do your work.

The next thing that we need to take a look at is what is going to make some good data visualization? These are created when we can add together design, data science, and communication all in one. Data visualization, when it is done right, can offer us some key insights into the sets of data that are complicated. This is done in a manner that makes them more meaningful and more intuitive overall for people using them.

Many companies can benefit from this kind of data visualization, and it is a tool that you do not want to overlook. Any time that you are trying to analyze your data and make sure that it matches well and that you are fully comprehending all of the information that is being shared, it is a good idea to look at some of the plots later on and decide which ones can talk about your data the best, and which one you should use.

You may be able to get all of the information that you need out of your data, and you may be able to complete your data analysis, without needing to have these charts. However, when you have a lot of data, you don't want to miss anything, and you don't have time to go through it all, these visuals will help. The best kinds of data visualizations will include plenty of complex ideas that can be communicated in a manner that has efficiency, precision, and clarity, to name a few.

To help you to craft a good kind of data visualization, you need to make sure that your data is clean, well-sourced, and complete.

This is a process that we did earlier in this guidebook, so your data should be prepared by this time. Once you are ready and the data is prepared, it is time to look over some of the charts and plots that are available to use. This is sometimes hard and a bit tricky based on the kind of information that you are working with at the time. You have to go with the chart type that seems to work best for the data that you have available.

After you have done some research and figured out which of the types of charts is the best, it is time to go through, design, as well as customize that chosen visual to work the best for you. Always keep the graphs and charts as simple as possible because these often make the best types of graphs. You do not want to take the time adding in a bunch of distracting elements that are not needed.

At this point, the visualization should be complete. You have picked out the one that you want to use after sorting through and cleaning your chosen data of course. Then, pick out the right chart to use, bringing in the code that goes with it to get the best results. Now that this part is done, it is time to take that visualization, publish and share it with others as well.

The PyTorch Library

The next library that we need to look at is known as PyTorch. This is a Python-based package that works for scientific computing.

It is going to rely on the power that it can receive from graphics processing units. This library is also going to be one of the most common and the preferred deep learning platforms for research to provide us with maximum flexibility and a lot of speed in the process.

There are plenty of benefits that come with this library. It is known for providing two of the most high-level features out of all the other deep learning libraries. These will include tensor computation with the support of a strong GPU acceleration, along with being able to build up the deep neural networks on an autograd system that is tape-based. There are many different libraries through Python that can help us work with a lot of artificial intelligence and deep learning projects that we want to work with. The PyTorch library is one of these. One of the key reasons that this library is so successful is because it is completely Pythonic and one that can take some of the models that you want to build with a neural network almost effortlessly. This is a newer deep learning library to work with, but there is a lot of momentum in this field as well.

The Beginnings of PyTorch

Even though it was just released in January 2016, it has become one of the go-to libraries that data scientists like to work with, mainly because it can make it easy to build complex neural networks. This is perfect for countless beginners who haven't been able to work with these neural networks at all in the past.

They can work with PyTorch and make their network in no time at all, even with a limited amount of coding experience.

The creators of this Python library envisioned that this library would be imperative when they wanted to run plentiful numerical computations as quickly as possible. This is one of the ideal methodologies that also fits in perfectly with the programming style that we see with Python. This library, along with the Python library, allowed debuggers of neural networks, machine learning developers, and deep learning scientists to not only run but also to test parts of their code in real-time. This is great news because it means that these professionals no longer have to wait for the entire code to complete and execute before they can check out whether this code works or if they need to fix certain parts.

In addition to some of the functions that comes with the PyTorch library, remember that you can extend out some of the functions of this library by adding in other Python packages. Python packages like Cython, SciPy, and NumPy all work well with PyTorch as well.

Even with these benefits, we still may have some questions about why the PyTorch library is so special, and why we may want to use this when it is time to build up the needed models for deep learning. The answer to this is simple: PyTorch is seen as a dynamic library.

This means that the library is flexible, and you can use it with any requirements and changes that you would like. It is so good at doing this job that it is being used by developers in artificial intelligence, and by students and researchers in many industries. In fact, in a Kaggle competition, this library was used by almost all of the individuals who finished in the top ten.

While there are multiplied benefits that can come with the PyTorch library, we need to start with some of the highlights of why professionals of all sorts love this language so much.

The interface is simple to use

The PyTorch interface is going to offer us an API that is easy to use. This means that we will find it simple to operate and run it as we do Python.

It is Pythonic in nature

This library, which is Pythonic, will smoothly integrate to work with the Python data science stack. Those who do not want to work with other coding languages along the way and want to just stick with the basics and some of the power of Python can do so with this library.

You will get the leverage of using all of the functions and services that are offered through the environment of Python.

Computational graphs

Another highlight that comes with the PyTorch library is that it provides us with a platform with some dynamic computational graphs. This means that you can change these graphs even during runtime. This is useful any time that you need to work on some graphs and you are not sure how much memory you need to use while creating this model for a neural network.

The Community for PyTorch

The next thing that we need to look at here is some of the community that comes with the PyTorch library. Because of all the benefits that come with PyTorch, we can see that the community of developers and other professionals is growing daily. In just a few years, this library has shown many developments, which has even led this library to be cited in many research papers and groups. When it comes to artificial intelligence and models of deep learning, PyTorch is starting to become one of the main libraries to work with.

One of the interesting things that come with PyTorch is that it is still in the early-release beta stage. But because so many programmers are adopting the framework for deep learning already and at such a brisk pace, it already shows the power and the potential that comes with it and how the community is likely to continue growing. For example, even though we are still on the beta release with PyTorch, there are currently 741 contributors just on the GitHub repository right now. This means that more than 700 people are working to enhance and add some improvements to the functions of PyTorch that are already there.

Think of how amazing this is! PyTorch is not technically released yet; it is still in the early stages. However, there has been so much buzz around this deep learning library, and so many programmers have been using it for deep learning and artificial intelligence, that there are already a ton of contributors who are working on adding more functions and improvements to this library for others to work with.

PyTorch is not going to limit the specific applications that we are working with because of the modular design and the flexibility that comes with it. It has seen heavy use by some of the leading tech giants; you may even recognize some of the names. Those who have already started to work with PyTorch to improve their deep learning models include Uber, NVIDIA, Twitter, and Facebook. This library has also been used in many domains for research, including neural networks, image recognition, translation, and NLP, among other key areas.

Why Use PyTorch with the Data Analysis

Anyone who is working in the field of data science, data analysis, artificial intelligence, or deep learning has likely spent some time working with the TensorFlow library, which we have talked about in this guidebook. TensorFlow may be the most popular library from Google, but because of the PyTorch framework for deep learning, we can find that this library can solve a few new problems when it comes to research work that these professionals want to fix.

It is often believed that PyTorch is now the biggest competitor out there to TensorFlow when it comes to handling data, and it is one of the best and most favorite artificial intelligence and deep learning library when it comes to the community of research. There are many reasons for this happening, and we will talk about some of these below.

First, we will notice that the dynamic computational graphs are popular among researchers. This library is going to avoid some of the static graphs that can be used in other frameworks from TensorFlow. This allows researchers and developers to change how the network is at the last minute. Some of those adopting this library will like it because these graphs are more intuitive to learn when we compare it to what TensorFlow can do.

The second benefit is that this one comes with a different kind of backend support. PyTorch is going to use a different backend based on what you are doing. The GPU, CPU, and other functional features will all come with a different backend, rather than focusing on just one backend to handle all of these. For example, we will see the THC for our GPU, and the TH for CPU.

Being able to use separate backends can make it easier for us to deploy this library through a variety of constrained systems. The imperative style is another benefit of working with this kind of library. This means that when we work with this library, it is easy to use and very intuitive. When you execute a line of code, it is going to get executed just as you want, and you can work with tracking that is in real-time. This allows the programmer to keep track of how the models for neural networks are doing. Because of the excellent architecture and the lean and fast approach, we have been able to increase some of the overall adoptions that we are seeing with this library throughout the communities of programmers. Another benefit that we will enjoy when it comes to working with PyTorch is that it is easy to extend. This library, in particular, is integrated to work well with the code for C++ and it is going to share a bit of the backend with this language when we work on our framework for deep learning. This means that a programmer cannot only use Python for the CPU and GPU, but he can also add in the extension of the API using the C or the C++ languages. This means that we can extend the usage of PyTorch for some of the new and experimental cases, which can make it even better when we want to do some research with it. Finally, the last benefit that we will focus on here is that PyTorch is seen as a Python approach library. This is because the library is a native Python package just by the way that it is designed. The functions that come with this are built as classes in Python, which means that all of the code that you write here can integrate seamlessly with the modules and packages of Python. Similar to what we see with NumPy, this Python-based library will enable us to work on a tensor that is GPU-accelerated, with computations that provide us with some rich options for APIs while applying a neural network. PyTorch is going to provide us with the research framework that we need from one end to another, which will come with most of the different building blocks that we need to carry out the research of deep learning on a day-to-day basis. We also notice that this library is going to provide us with high-level neural network modules because it can work with an API that is similar to the Keras library as well.

Pandas

Pandas are built on NumPy and they are meant to be used together. This makes it extremely easy to extract arrays from the data frames. Once these arrays are extracted, they can be turned into data frames themselves. Let's take a look at an example:

In: import pandas as pd

import numpy as np

marketing_filename = 'regression-datasets-marketing.csv'

marketing = pd.read_csv(marketing _filename, header=None)

In this phase, we are uploading data to a data frame. Next, we're going to use the "values" method to extract an array that is of the same type as those contained inside the data frame.

In: marketing_array = marketing.values

marketing_array.dtype

Out: dtype('float64')

We can see that we have a float type array. You can anticipate the type of the array by first using the "dtype" method. This will establish which types are being used by the specified data frame object. Do this before extracting the array. This is how this operation would look:

In: marketing.dtypes

Out: 0float64

1int64

2float64

3int64

4float64

5float64

6float64

7float64

8int64

9int64

10int64

11float64

12float64

13float64

dtype: object

Matrix Operations

This includes matrix calculations, such as matrix-to-matrix multiplication. Let's create a two-dimensional array.

This is a two-dimensional array of numbers from 0 to 24. Next, we will declare a vector of coefficients and a column that will stack the vector and its reverse. Here's what it would look like:

In: coefs = np.array([1., 0.5, 0.5, 0.5, 0.5])

coefs_matrix = np.column_stack((coefs,coefs[::-1]))

print (coefs_matrix)

Out:

[[1. 0.5]

[0.50.5]

[0.50.5]

[0.50.5]

[0.51.]]

In: np.dot(M,coefs)

Out: array([5.,20.,35.,50.,65.])

Here's an example of multiplication between the array and the coefficient vectors:

In: np.dot(M,coefs_matrix)

Out: array([[5.,7.],

[20.,22.],

[35.,37.],

[50.,52.],

[65.,67.]])

In both of these multiplication operations, we used the "np.dot" function to achieve them.

Slicing and Indexing

Indexing is great for viewing the nd-array by sending an instruction to visualize the slice of columns and rows or the index.

Let's start by creating a 10 x 10 array. It will initially be two-dimensional.

In: import numpy as np

M = np.arange(100, dtype=int).reshape(10,10)

Next, let's extract the rows from 2 to 8, but only the ones that are evenly numbered.

In: M[2:9:2,:]

Out: array([[20, 21, 22, 23, 24, 25, 26, 27, 28, 29],

[40, 41, 42, 43, 44, 45, 46, 47, 48, 49],

[60, 61, 62, 63, 64, 65, 66, 67, 68, 69],

[80, 81, 82, 83, 84, 85, 86, 87, 88, 89]])

Now let's extract the column, but only the ones from index 5.

In: M[2:9:2,5:]

Out: array([[25, 26, 27, 28, 29],

[45, 46, 47, 48, 49],

[65, 66, 67, 68, 69],

[85, 86, 87, 88, 89]])

We successfully sliced the rows and the columns. But what happens if we try a negative index? Doing so would reverse the array. Here's how our previous array would look when using a negative index.

In: M[2:9:2,5::-1]

Out: array([[25, 24, 23, 22, 21, 20],

[45, 44, 43, 42, 41, 40],

[65, 64, 63, 62, 61, 60],

[85, 84, 83, 82, 81, 80]])

However, keep in mind that this process is only a way of viewing the data. If you want to use these views further by creating new data, you cannot make any modifications to the original arrays. If you do, it can lead to some negative side effects. In that case, you want to use the "copy" method. This will create a copy of the array, which you can modify however you wish. Here's the code line for the copy method:

In: N = M[2:9:2,5:].copy()

The next option that we need to take a look at is a bit of the work that we can do with the Pandas library. This is one of the most important libraries that we can work with overall, because it can handle pretty much all of the parts that come with data analysis. There isn't anything in data analysis that the Pandas library won't be able to help us out with. Pandas are one of the packages from Python that can provide us with numerous different tools to help in data analysis. The package is going to come with a lot of different structures of data that can be used for the different tasks that we need to do to manipulate our data. It is also going to come with a lot of methods that we can invoke for the analysis, which is really useful when we are ready to work on some of our machine learning and data science projects in this language.

As we can imagine already, there are several benefits that we can enjoy when we work with the Pandas library, especially when compared to some of the other options out there. First, it is going to present for our data in a manner that is suitable to handle all of our analysis through the different data structures, in particular through the DataFrame and the Series structures.

In addition to this, we will find that this is a package that can contain a lot of different methods that are convenient for data filtering and more. The Pandas library will come with a lot of the utilities that we need to perform operations of Input and Output seamlessly. And no matter which format your data is going to come to us in, whether it is CSV, MS Excel, or TSV, the Pandas library can handle it for us.

How to Install Pandas

When you work with the traditional Python distribution, you will find that it is not going to have the module of Pandas. You will need to go through the process of installing this to your computer to get it to work. The nice thing that you will quickly notice, though, is that Python is going to come with a tool that is known as pip, which is exactly what you want to use to install Pandas on your computer. To do this specific installation, we need to go through and use the command below:

$ pip install pandas

If you already have the Anaconda program on your system, then you need to use a slightly different command to help you out. This command is:

$ conda install pandas

It is often recommended that when you do this process, you go through and install the latest version of the Pandas package to get all of the new features and more that we need along the way. However, it is still possible to get some of the older versions, and you can install this one as well. You can just go through and specify which of the versions you would like to use when working on the conda install code that we did above.

<u>The Data Structures in Pandas</u>

With some of this in mind, it is time for us to go through a few of the different things that we can do with the Pandas code. First, we need to look at the data structures. There are two of these data structures that we can work with, including the series and the DataFrame.

The first one here is the series

This is similar to what we can work with when it comes to a one-dimensional array. It can go through and store data of any type. The values of a Pandas Series are mutable, but you will find that the size of our series is immutable, and we are not able to change them later.

The first element in this series is given an index of 0. Then the last element that is found in this kind of index is N-1, because N is the total number of elements that we put into our series. To create one of our own Series in Pandas, we need to first go through the process of importing the package of Pandas through the insert command of Python. The code we can use include the below.

Import pandas as pd

Then, we can go through and create one of our own Series. We will invoke the method of pd.Series() and then pass on the array. This is simple to work with. The code that we can use to help us work with this includes:

Series1 = pd.Series([1, 2, 3, 4])

We need to then work with the print statement in order to display the contents of the Series. You can see that when you run this one, you have two columns. The first one is the first one with numbers starting from the index of 0 like we talked about before, and then the second one is the different elements that we added to our series. The first column is going to denote the indices for the elements. However, you could end up with an error if you are working with the display Series. The major cause of this error is that the Pandas library is going to take some time to look for the amount of information that is displayed, this means that you need to provide the sys output information. You are also able to go through this with the help of a NumPy array, like we talked about earlier. This is why we need to make sure that when we are working with the Pandas library. We can also go through and install, and use the NumPy library as well. The second type of data structure that we can work with here will include the DataFrames. These will often come in as a table. It can organize the data into columns and rows, which is going to turn it into a two-dimensional data structure. This means that we have the potential to have columns that are of a different type, and the size of the DataFrame that we want to work with are mutable, and then it can be modified. To help us to work with this and create one of our own, we need to either go through and start a new one from scratch, or we will convert other data structures, like the arrays for NumPy into the DataFrame.

There are a lot of different parts that we can handle when it comes to the Pandas library. Getting this set up and ready to go for some of our own needs is important in this process as well.

this is one of the best libraries to work with when it is time to handle our work in Python code with data analysis. This can handle all of the different parts that come with the data analysis along the way.

Jupyter Notebook

The Jupyter Note pad is an open-source web application that permits you to produce and share files that contain live code, formulas, visualizations, and narrative text. It utilizes and consists of information cleansing and change, mathematical simulation, analytical modeling, information visualization, artificial intelligence, and far more.

Jupyter has assistance for over 40 various languages, and Python is among them. Python is a requirement (Python 3.3 or higher, or Python 2.7) for setting up the Jupyter Notebook itself.

Setting up Jupyter utilizing Anaconda

Set up Python and Jupyter utilizing the Anaconda Distribution, which includes Python, the Jupyter Notebook, and other typically utilized bundles for clinical computing and information science. You can download Anaconda's newest Python 3 variation.

Now, set up the downloaded variation of Anaconda.

Setting up Jupyter Notebook utilizing PIP:

python3 -m pip install --upgrade pip

python3 -m pip install jupyter

Command to run the Jupyter notebook:

jupyter notebook

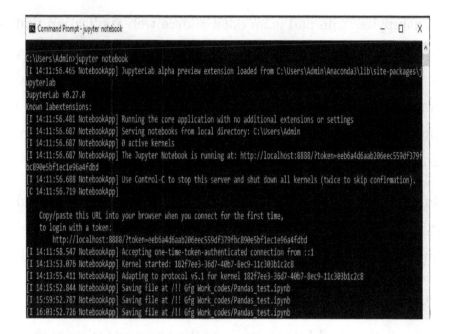

When the Notepad opens in your Internet browser, you will see the notebook dashboard, which will reveal a list of the notepads, files, and subdirectories in the directory site where the Notepad server was started.

The majority of the time, you will want to begin a Notepad server in the greatest level directory site consisting of notepads.

Typically, this are your house directory site.

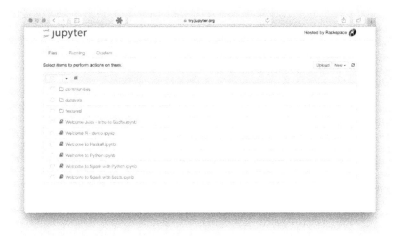

Create a new Notebook

Now on the control panel, you can see a brand-new button at the top-right corner. Click it to open a drop-down list. After that, if you'll click Python 3, it will open a brand-new notebook.

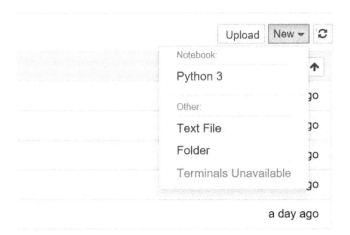

Running Your First code in Jupyter

Action #1: After effectively setting up Jupyter, compose 'jupyter note pad' in the terminal/command timely. This will open a brand-new Notepad server on your Internet browser.

Action #2: On the leading left corner, click the brand-new button and choose Python 3. This will open a brand-new Notepad tab in your Web browser where you can begin to compose your very first code.

Action #3: Press **Click** or get in on the very first cell in your Notepad to enter into the edit mode.

Action #4: Now you are free to compose any code.

Action #5: You can run your code by pushing **Shift** + **Enter** or the Run button offered at the top. An example code is provided listed below:

```
In [6]:  # Define a function for addition
         def add(a , b):
             return a + b

         val = add(12, 13)

         val

Out[6]:  25
```

Jupyter Notebook Tips and Tricks

Python is a fantastic language for doing information analysis, mainly because of the great environment of data-centric Python bundles. What makes information analysis in Python more efficient and effective is Jupyter Notepad or what was previously called the IPython Notepad. In this area, we will go over some great functions of the Jupyter Notepad, which increases the efficiency and effectiveness of the information expert. The Jupyter Notepad extends the console-based technique to interactive computing in qualitatively brand-new instructions, offering a web-based application appropriate for recording the entire calculation procedure: establishing, recording, and carrying out code, along with interacting outcomes. In a nutshell, it is a total plan. Let's see some functions of the Jupyter Notepad, which becomes extremely convenient while doing information analysis.

%%timeit and %%time

It's not an unusual thing for an information researcher that while doing information analysis, they have more than one service for the provided issue. They wish to pick the very best technique, which accomplishes the job in the minimum quantity of time. Jupyter Notepad supplies an extremely effective method to inspect the running time of a specific block of code.

We can utilize the %% time command to inspect the running time of a specific cell. Let's see the time takes to carry out the code pointed out listed below.

```
# For capturing the execution time

%%time

# Find the squares of a number in the

# range from 0 to 14

for x in range(15):

square = x**2

print(square)
```

Output:

```
0
1
4
9
16
25
36
49
64
81
100
121
144
169
196
Wall time: 999 µs
```

We can likewise utilize the command %%timeit to run the provided bit of code over many times to discover the typical run time for that piece of code.

Commenting/Uncommenting a block of code:

While dealing with codes, we typically include brand-new lines of code and comment out the old pieces of code for enhancing the efficiency or to debug it.

Jupyter Notepad supplies an extremely effective method to accomplish the same – to comment out a block of code.

We require to choose all those lines which we want to comment out, as shown in the following picture:

```
 1  df = pd.DataFrame({'Date':['10/2/2011','11/2/2011','12/2/2011','13/2/2011'],
 2                     'Event':['Music','Poetry','Theatre','Comedy'],
 3                     'Cost':[10000,5000,15000,2000]})
 4
 5  df.index = ['A', 'B', 'A', 'D']
 6
 7  print(df)
 8
 9  df2 = pd.DataFrame({'Cost1':[10025,5700,2415,1800],
10                      'Cost2':[1000,500,150,20],
11                      'Cost3':[10000,5000,15000,2000]})
12
13  print(df.columns)
```

Next, on a Windows computer system, we need to push the **Ctrl** + / crucial mix to comment out the highlighted part of the code.

```
|:  1  df = pd.DataFrame({'Date':['10/2/2011','11/2/2011','12/2/2011','13/2/2011'],
    2                     'Event':['Music','Poetry','Theatre','Comedy'],
    3                     'Cost':[10000,5000,15000,2000]})
    4
    5  df.index = ['A', 'B', 'A', 'D']
    6
    7  # print(df)
    8
    9  # df2 = pd.DataFrame({'Cost1':[10025,5700,2415,1800],
   10  #                     'Cost2':[1000,500,150,20],
   11  #                     'Cost3':[10000,5000,15000,2000]})
   12
   13  print(df.columns)
```

This does conserve a great deal of time for the information expert.

Next, on a Windows computer system, we need to push the **Ctrl** + / crucial mix to comment out the highlighted part of the code.

```
:  1  df = pd.DataFrame({'Date':['10/2/2011','11/2/2011','12/2/2011','13/2/2011'],
   2                     'Event':['Music','Poetry','Theatre','Comedy'],
   3                     'Cost':[10000,5000,15000,2000]})
   4
   5  df.index = ['A', 'B', 'A', 'D']
   6
   7  print(df)
   8
   9  df2 = pd.DataFrame({'Cost1':[10025,5700,2415,1800],
  10                      'Cost2':[1000,500,150,20],
  11                      'Cost3':[10000,5000,15000,2000]})
  12
  13  print(df.columns)
```

Chapter 5:

How to process and understand data

Data Life Cycle

One of the most important things that we can do when it is time to combine data science and Python into one is learning a bit more about the data life cycle. There are a lot of steps that we need to take before we can take our data and learn something from it. Many people and companies who want to get into the process of using their data to make decisions assume that they can just look around for a bit of data, and then find the insights all at once.

Let's take a look at some of the main steps that companies need to follow in the life cycle of their data to ensure they get the best results possible:

Gathering our Data

The first thing that we need to do is find all of that data that we would like to use in the first place. This is a critical step because we are not going to be able to create a model and learn a lot of the predictions and the insights that we would like if there isn't any data for us to sort through in the first place. This is a very important step to take because it ensures that we not only have a lot of data, but we also have the data that we would like to use to find the answers to our biggest questions.

To start, we need to be able to go through and figure out what business question we would like to have answered. We are not just randomly looking through some of the data that is there and hoping that we can figure out something. We have way too much data to sort through when it comes to this, and it is not going to end well for us if we are doing this. Instead, we need to spend some time thinking about what our biggest business problems are, and what we would like to gain when we go through this data.

Preparing the Data

The next thing that we need to spend some time on is preparing the data that we want to use. It is likely that you went through and collected the data that is used in your model and some of your decisions, later on, will come from a variety of sources. And this is going to make things messy. The results that you get from a survey that you sent out are different compared to the results that you get from your social media account.

Both of these can be useful when it is time to work with data science, but they will present a few challenges to you. This does mean that we need to be able to prepare the data and get it all cleaned and organized ahead of time to avoid confusion and ensure that our model can handle it.

During this particular phase, we will need to work with something that is known as an **analytical sandbox**. This is a place where you can perform some of the different analytics that you want to use for the whole time that you handle your project. There are a lot of steps that you need to take while working on your data before you are ever able to do the modeling, which we will focus on later on.

Model Planning

Once we have had some time to go through and collect our raw data from different sources, and we have prepared and cleaned the data so that it is ready to use, it is time for us to move on to the third phase of this process: model planning. In this phase, we will spend some time figuring out which techniques and methods are the best to draw the relationships between the variables.

These relationships are important and we need to spend some time looking into them and understanding how they work a bit better. In fact, these relationships can set up some of the bases that we need for our algorithms to work, and that is definitely going to affect the next phase as it is implemented. It is during this phase that we can apply the Exploratory Data Analysis (EDA) with the help of a lot of different visualization tools and the statistical formulas that we want to use in this process.

Build the Model

Now that we have had a chance to talk about planning the model and the different tools and techniques that we can use to make this happen, it is time for us build this model. This is a process that is going to take some time, and we need to make sure that we can spend our time training and testing the model as well, to ensure that it will provide us with some of the accurate results that we are looking for.

When we are working on this phase, we will work with two distinct data sets, one for training and one for testing. You will also need to take some time to do a bit of exploration to figure out whether or not the existing tools that we are using are enough to help us run our models on it, or if we would like to work with a more robust environment in the process. You will need to take some time here to analyze the various learning techniques including clustering, classification, and association to help us build a model.

Operationalize

Now that the model has had some time to be built up and we are sure that the information that it provides us, such as the predictions and the insights that we are hoping to use, are as accurate as possible, it is time for us to use the model to help us out.

Here we can take some time to put in our data and let the model do its work helping us to see the predictions and insights that will come out of that data as well.

In this phase, we will gather up the insights and the predictions that we need, and then use them as a way to make some important decisions for the business. It is important here to work with the technical documents, code, briefings, and final reports on the findings that you were able to get out of the process.

In some cases, this is taken a bit further. Depending on the business process that you would like to work with, it may help to do a pilot project, one that we can implement in real-time, to help us learn whether the insights and the predictions that we get out of this model are good for us, or if they need some adjustments before we implement them throughout the whole company. This is going to still be a part of the process because we can use these findings to help bolster up some of the other parts that we want to work with.

Communicate the Results

The final step that we need to take a look at here is to communicate the results that we are seeing. We have gone through a lot of steps already with our data and with some of the machine learning algorithms. We have made some good headway in the process as well.

Now that we know some of these insights and perhaps even have a good idea of whether some of them will work in real life or not, it is time to communicate the results.

It is unlikely that the data scientist or the one who is actually going through this process and creating and working with the algorithms is the one who uses that information. Instead, they are supposed to find that information and then present it to some of the key decision-makers in the company to help those top people figure things out. That is exactly where this step of the process is going to come into play.

Now it is important to take some time in this part of the process to evaluate what information we were able to find inside of the data, and then evaluate if we have been able to achieve the goals that we would have liked to meet in the first stage of this process.

So, for this last phase that we are in right now, it is our goal to go through and identify all of the various key findings that showed up in the data that we have, and in all of the information that we are working with, and figure out how to communicate all of this information to the key stakeholders. Then together, or with just the key people who make decisions for that business, you can determine whether or not the results that were found in the project were a success or failure.

Completing the Data Analysis

While we are on the topic of working with data science, we also need to take a look at some of the data analysis. This is an important part of all the work that we will do with the help of a data science project. It is the part that you have probably been waiting for so far in this process. This is basically a subset of data science, and it is where we will handle the data that we are gathering, which comes in from many different sources, and then using algorithms to help us figure out what all of this data means.

You can use all of the data that we want, and we can fill up many data warehouses if we would like. But if you don't understand what the data is telling us, then the data is not going to matter all that much, and your company will not be able to use it. This is where we can grab the process of data analysis and make it come into play.

To help us get started, data analytics will take the raw data that we have and then analyze it to help us make some good conclusions about raw information.

When the techniques of data analytics are used appropriately, data analysis can help us see some of the metrics and the trends that we may miss out on in some of the other situations out there in a sea of so much data. This information is then going to be what we can use to optimize processes to help increase how efficient a system or a business can be, overall.

Now that we know a bit about the broad meaning of data analytics, it is time to get into some of the different parts of it, and how we can use it to our advantage. The term data analytics is broad, and it includes many diverse types of data analysis. Any type of information that can be subjected to techniques of data analytics to get inside that can then be used by humans to improve something about their business will fall under this umbrella.

Following the right steps along the way can make a big difference in what we will see with this data analysis. Some of the different steps that we can use here will include the following:

We start this process by determining the requirements of the data or how the data has been grouped. There are a lot of possibilities here, including the data being separated by things like gender, income, demographics, and age. The values of the data could also be numerical, or they may be divided up by category as well.

The second step of this is the process of collecting our data. There are a ton of different sources where you can get all of this information. It could be from your employees, from sources in the environment, online sources like surveys and social media, and even from your computer system.

Once the data has been collected, and you are sure you have the data that you need, it is time to organize the data. Since you are collecting it from a variety of sources, you have to make sure that it is organized in a manner that makes sense, and one that the algorithm can read through quickly and find the trends to make predictions from when you get to that step.

You can choose what method you would like to use when you organize the information. You can work with a spreadsheet or try some kind of software that is good at handling statistical data. Once you have been able to organize the data the way that you would like, it is time to clean it all up before the analysis happens. This means that the data scientist has to scrub the data and check that there are no errors or duplications in the information, or that the data is not incomplete. This step takes some time, but it ensures that everything is fixed and ready to go before you even start. The key thing that we have to remember here is that it is the science that we can use to use raw data, analyze it, and then draw some good conclusions on this information as well. The processes and the techniques that are used in this kind of thing are automated in many cases, and you will see that when we work with the right algorithm, it can turm raw data into something that humans can consume. The main reason that a business would want to use this kind of process to analyze the data is because it is useful in optimizing your customer service and performance.

<u>Why Does the Analysis of Data Matter?</u>

While we are here, we need to take a moment to look at why this data analysis is so important, and why a business would like to go through these algorithms and more to learn from that data they have been able to gather in the first place. These companies find that they can use the insights and predictions that are in the data, but when there is such a large amount of data, and all of that data comes to them from a variety of sources, it is going to need a lot of work to sort through. Too much work to try and do manually.

The process of data analytics is something that can be helpful to any business whatever the industry they are in because it will help them to optimize their performance. It can also help them to work on their business model and can make it easier for them to identify methods that are more efficient in reducing costs and getting things figured out.

In addition to all of this, a company can take data analysis and make decisions that will help propel them into future success. Analysis is also going to help them to learn more about some of the customer trends that are out there and can help to offer new services and products that will work for your customers as well.

Choices in Data Analysis

The next thing that we need to spend some of our time on is to figure out what kinds of analyses are open for you to work with as well. There are a lot of variations that come with the data analysis, and you can pick the one that works the best for your needs. There are a number of these, but we will focus on some of the ones that you are most likely to use when you first get started on this whole process. The four basic types that a beginner in data analysis can focus on, and that most data scientists will work with will include the following:

Descriptive analytics

This is one that will take the time to describe what has happened in the data over a chosen period. You may look at things like whether the number of views has gone up, or if the sales for your company are higher or lower than they were in the previous month for a product.

Diagnostic analytics

This is the one that will focus more on why something has happened or on the roots of your business. This is helpful but it will involve data inputs that are more diverse and a bit of hypothesizing in the process. For example, did you have a slow sales week because the weather was bad and no one went out shopping? Or did something go wrong with one of your marketing campaigns, and that is why sales are struggling?

Predictive analytics

This one is used to help predict what is most likely to happen in the near future based on the information that we have at our disposal right now. What happened to the sales last year when the summer was warm?

How many weather models will tell us that there are a hot summer this year, and we should prepare for more of what we saw in the past?

Prescriptive analytics

This one is responsible for suggesting a course of action that the company should take. For example, if the likelihood of a hot summer is measured as an average of five weather models and this likelihood is above 58 percent, then it is likely that you should add in more shifts to handle the sales if this is something that has happened in the past.

Even without a professional with this, companies can learn how to make the data analysis work and can then use this to leverage a ton of data and learn from it. Companies are seeing all of the benefits of doing this. They like that this is going to help them to make some smart decisions, ones that are driven by data so that they can see a lot of benefits and see how to beat the competition.

What Are the Benefits of a Data Analysis?

When it is time to work with data analysis, it will not take you too long to realize that there are a lot of benefits that will come with this overall as well. No matter what kind of company you are in and what your goals are, you can receive a lot of these benefits in the process as well. This process may seem like it has a ton of steps and that you will spend too long working on for it to be worth your time. But it can be so worth it if you take the time to learn about the data and all of the cool things that it can do for you. With this in mind, some of the benefits that you will receive when it is time to work with data analysis for your company, no matter what kind of company, will include the following factors.

It helps you to understand your customers better

All businesses want to understand their customers. This is the best way to make more sales and increase revenue. But how are you supposed to know what the customer wants, and what is going to convince them to come to your store compared to going over to a competitor? This data analysis can take information from customer surveys and customer habits and help you make more informed decisions to provide better customer service to increase sales.

It helps you to find trends that you should follow for your business

There are always trends that go on in any market, but these trends are often shifting and changing at really fast rates that are hard to keep up with. Using data analysis can help you to catch on to some of the trends ahead of time, making it easier for you to meet the needs of your customers.

It helps you to know your product better

Sometimes, data analysis can be used to help you know which products are doing the best and why. You may find out that one product is actually doing better than you thought, or that you should start selling more of a similar product to increase sales.

It can help make smarter business decisions overall

It is always best if you can have data and information behind all of the decisions that you make for your company. The data analysis helps you to comb through all of that information and see what is there before you make any decisions about your company.

Data analysis is one of the best ways that you can beat the competition

Companies who are willing to look through the data and are willing to see what insights and trends are there are the ones who can find these things faster than the competition, and who can win in their industry.

You will find that these benefits will help out your company, and are some of the main reasons why this data analysis can be so good for the whole company, and why it is something that is in such high demand for almost every industry that is out there. For some of the smaller companies that are out there, the ones who may not be choosing to work with this kind of process will find that they can still work with it on a local level and get some results as well.

There are so many benefits that will come with your data analysis, and being able to figure out how to make this happens, and what you can do to see some of the results when it comes to learning what is in that data, is very important as well.

Data Visualization

This is a unique part of our data science journey, and it is so important that we spend some time and effort looking through it and understanding what this process is all about. Data visualization is so important when it comes to our data analysis. It can take all of the complex relationships that we have been focusing on in our analysis and puts them in a graph format, or at least in another visual format that is easier to look through.

Sometimes, looking at all of those numbers and figures can be boring and hard to concentrate on. It can take a long time for us to figure out what relationships are present and which ones we should ignore. But when we put the information into some kind of graph form, such as a graph, a chart, or something similar, then we can easily see some of the complex relationships that show up, and the information will make more sense overall.

Many of those who are in charge of making decisions based on that data and on the analysis that you have worked on will appreciate having a graph or another tool in place to help them out.

Having the rest of the information in place as well can make a difference and can back up what you are saying, but having that graph in place is one of the best ways to ensure that they can understand the data and the insights that you have found.

To make it simple, data visualization is the presentation of data that shows up in a graphical or a pictorial format of some kind or another. It is going to enable those who make big decisions for a business to see the analytics presented more visually so that they can grasp some of the more difficult concepts or find some new patterns out of the data that they would never have known in any other manner.

There are a lot of different options that you can work with when it comes to data visualization and having it organized and ready to go the way that you like, using the right tools along the way, can make life easier.

With an interactive visual, you can take this concept a bit further and use technology to drill down the information, while interactively changing what data is shown and how it is processed for you.

Why Is Data Visualization So Important?

The next thing that we need to take a look at here is why data visualization is so important to us. The reason that data visualization is something that we want to spend our time and energy on is because of the way that someone can process information. It is hard to gather all of the important insights and more on a process when we have to just read it off a table or a piece of paper. Sure, the information is all right there, but sometimes it is still hard to form the conclusions and actually see what we are doing when it is just in text format for us.

For most people, being able to look at a chart or a graph or some other kind of visual can make things a little bit easier.

Because of the way that our brains work and process the information that we see, using graphs and charts to visualize a large amount of complex data is so much easier compared to pouring over some reports or spreadsheets. When we work with data visualization, we will find that it is a quick and easy way to convey a lot of hard and challenging concepts, usually in a more universal manner. We can experiment with different scenarios by using an interactive visual that can make some slight adjustments when we need them the most. This is just the beginning of what data visualization can do for us though, and we will likely find more and more uses for this as time goes on.

Some of the other ways that data visualization can help us out will include:

- Identify areas that will need the most attention when it comes to improvements and attention.

- Help us to figure out which of our products we should place where.

- It can clarify which factors are the most likely to influence the behavior of a customer.

- It can make it easier to tell and make predictions about our sales volumes, whether these volumes are higher or lower at a specific time.

The process of data visualization is going to help us change up the way that we can work with the data that we are using.

Data analysis is supposed to respond to any issues that are found in the company in a faster manner than ever before.

They need to be able to dig through and find more insights as well, look at data differently and learn how to be more imaginative and creative in the process.

This is exactly something that data visualization can help us out with.

How Can We Use Data Visualization?

The next thing that we need to take some time to look at is how companies throughout many industries can use data visualization for their own needs. No matter the size of the company or what kind of industry they are in, it is possible to use some of the basics of data visualization to help make more sense of the data at hand. There are a variety of ways that data visualization can help you succeed.

The first benefit that we can look at is the fact that these visuals are a great way for us to comprehend the information that we see in a faster fashion. When we can use a graphical representation of all that data on our business, rather than reading through charts and spreadsheets, we can see these large amounts of data clearly and cohesively.

It is much easier to go through all of that information and see what is found inside, rather than having to try to guess and draw the conclusions on our own.

Since it is often much faster for us to analyze this kind of information in a graphical format, rather than analyzing it on a spreadsheet, it becomes easier for us to understand what is there. When we can do it in this manner, it is so much easier for a business to address problems or answer some of their big questions promptly, so that things are fixed without issue or without having to worry about more damage.

The second benefit that comes with using data visuals to help out with the process of data science is that they can make it easy to pinpoint some of the emerging trends that we need to focus on. This information is within the data, and we can find it even if we just read through the spreadsheets and the documents.

However, this takes a lot of time, can be boring, and often it is hard for us to see these correlations and relationships. We may miss out on some of the more important information that we need. Using the idea of these visuals to handle the data and discover trends, whether this is the trends just in the individual business or in the market as a whole, can help to ensure that your business gains some big advantages over others in your competition base. Of course, any time that you can beat the competition, it is going to positively affect your bottomline.

When you use the right visual to help you get the work done, it is much easier to spot some of the outliers that are presen—the ones that are more likely to affect the quality of your product, the customer churn, or other factors that will change your business. Also, it is going to help you to address issues before they can turn into much bigger problems that you have to work with.

Next on the list is that these visuals can help you identify some relationships and patterns that are found in all of that data that you are using.

Even with extensive amounts of data that is complicated, we can find that the information starts to make more sense when it is presented in a graphic format, rather than in just a spreadsheet or another format.

With the visuals, it becomes so much easier for a business to recognize some of the different parameters that are there and how these are highly correlated with one another. Some of the correlations that we can see within our data are pretty obvious, but there are others that won't be as obvious. When we use these visuals to help us find and know about these relationships, it is going to make it much easier for our business to focus on the areas that are the most likely to influence some of our most important goals.

We may also find that working with these visuals can help us to find some of the outliers in the information that is there. Sometimes these outliers mean nothing. If you are looking at the charts and graphs and find just a few random outliers that don't seem to connect, it is best to cut these out of the system and not worry about them.

However, there are times when these outliers are important and we should pay more attention to them.

If you are looking at some of the visuals that you have and you notice that there are a substantial amount of them that fall in the same area, then you will need to pay closer attention. This could be an area that you can focus your attention on to reach more customers—a problem that could grow into a major challenge if you are not careful or turn into something else that you need to pay some attention to.

These visuals can also help us to learn more about our customers. We can use them to figure out where our customers are, what kinds of products our customers would be the happiest with, how we can provide better services to our customers, and more. Many companies decide to work with data visualization to help them learn more about their customers and to ensure that they can stand out from the crowd with the work they do.

Now, we could just hand these individuals, the ones who make some of the big decisions, the spreadsheets, and some of the reports that we have. They will probably be able to learn a lot of information from that. But this is not always the best way to do things.

Instead, we need to make sure that we set things up with the help of a visual, ensuring that these individuals who make the big decisions can look it over and see some of the key relationships and information at a glance.

Using graphs, charts, and some of the other visuals that are impactful as a representation of our data is so important in this step because it is engaging and can help us to get our message across to others in a faster manner than before.

As we can see, there are a lot of benefits that come in when we talk about data visualizations and all of the things that we can do with them. Being able to figure out the best kind of visualization that works for your needs and ensuring that you can turn that data into a graph or chart or another visualization is so important when it is time to work with your data analysis.

We can certainly analyze without data visualization. But when it comes to showcasing the findings in an attractive and easy to understand format, nothing is better than data visualization.

Conclusion

Congratulations are in order as you successfully completed your fundamental training in data science. You came a long way from learning how to install your Python work environment. Sit back and allow time to solidify your knowledge because you have just processed a great deal of information. Data science isn't a light topic, and some of the techniques and algorithms you explored can be challenging.

Data science is a massive field of study that requires years of learning and practice before you can master it. This shouldn't discourage you, however! Embrace it as a challenge that you can undertake in order to broaden your horizons and improve your knowledge of all that is data science and machine learning. This book offers you the fundamental knowledge you need to get started. However, keep in mind that no book or even teacher can do everything for you. You need to work hard by putting each building block in its place as you advance.

Now that you have finished learning the basics, you should take the time to go over this book one more time to make sure you didn't overlook anything. It is vital that you understand the theory behind learning these algorithms and analysis techniques before you advance to the next stage. Take what you have learned so far, and make sure to practice every concept on your own with one of the widely available open-source datasets. By learning everything in a structured manner and applying it to practice, you can become a data scientist in no time!

The next step is to get started by seeing how data science can work for your business. You will find that there are a lot of different ways that you can use the large amount of information that you have access to, and all of the data that you have been able to collect over time. Collecting the data is just the first step to the process. We also need to make sure that we can gain all of the insights and predictions that come out of that information, and this is where the process of data science is going to come into play.

However, this is not the only step that we can work with. We also need to take this a bit further and not just collect the data, but also be able to analyze that data and see what information it holds. This is a part of the data science life cycle, but it deserves some special attention because, without it, the data would just sit there without being used.

In this guidebook, we worked with the Python coding language and how this was able to help us to work through all of that data, collecting models and more, so we could learn something useful and make predictions about the data as well.

Data science is a great thing to add to your business, and it can help you to make sure customer satisfaction is high, that waste is low, that you can make more money, and can even help with predictions in the future, such as what products you should develop and put out on the market. But learning all of this is not something that just happens on its own. Working with data science and adding in Python language and different libraries that are included with it can make the difference. When you are ready to work with Python data science to improve many different aspects of your own business and to beat the competition, make sure to check out this guidebook to help you get started with it right away.

You don't necessarily need a computer science degree to learn all aspects of data science. What you do need, however, is that spark that urges you to learn more and put everything new to the test by working with real data sets and actual data science projects. Acquire more books and join online communities of data scientists, programmers, statisticians, and machine learning enthusiasts!

You can benefit a lot from working with others. Expose yourself to other perspectives and ideas as soon as possible, even when you barely know the basics. The learning process receives a boost when you have other people with similar goals helping you out.

Data science is a complex field that requires a lot of dedication from you due to the amount of information you need to absorb. This book hands you the tools you need to study every concept and guides you with clear examples of code and data sets. The rest is up to you! You have the fundamentals on your belt; now you can continue your journey to become a data scientist!